46 SWEET AND SAVORY RECIPES
for Pies, Jams, Smoothies, Sauces, and More

Blueberry Love

Cynthia Graubart

T0002191

Storey Publishing

To Anne and Heyward Siddons, beloved friends and chosen family.
For the love of all things Maine.

*The mission of Storey Publishing is to serve our customers by
publishing practical information that encourages
personal independence in harmony with the environment.*

Edited by Deanna F. Cook and Sarah Guare
Art direction and book design by Alethea Morrison
Text production by Liseann Karandisecky
Indexed by Christine R. Lindemer, Boston Road Communications
Cover and interior photography by © Keller + Keller Photography
Author photo (back cover flap) by Just Bartee Photography
Food and prop styling by Catrine Kelty

Storey books are available at special discounts
when purchased in bulk for premiums and
sales promotions as well as for fund-raising or
educational use. Special editions or book excerpts
can also be created to specification. For details,
please call 800-827-8673, or send an email to
sales@storey.com.

Storey Publishing
210 MASS MoCA Way
North Adams, MA 01247
storey.com

Printed in China through World Print
10 9 8 7 6 5 4 3 2 1

Library of Congress Cataloging-in-Publication
Data on file

Contents

Introduction, 1

Tips for Cooking
  with Blueberries, 2

Cook's Notes, 4

BREAKFAST, 6

SALADS & SIDES, 33

LUNCH & DINNER, 49

DESSERT, 60

Acknowledgments, 98

Index, 99

INTRODUCTION

My love of blueberries began in the late 1980s, when I met a blueberry farmer in Gainesville, Florida, who was tilling the acidic, dry, and dusty soil in an effort to coax rabbiteye blueberry bushes into fruition. Blueberries were a brand-new agricultural endeavor for the state at the time, and I had little exposure to them. Now Florida is among the top 10 states producing commercial blueberries, and my love of these little blue superfruits is stronger than ever.

Not long after my encounter with the blueberry farmer, I started traveling to Maine in the summer, where I began picking wild berries from ancient blueberry barrens and baking them into cobblers, muffins, and pies. Each summer I return, I marvel at all the ways I can invent to cook with my beloved berry.

Wild Maine blueberries are native to North America. Primarily grown in the northeastern United States and Canada, they appeared in northern glacial soils nearly 10,000 years ago. But it's thanks to the work of Dr. Frederick Coville, a USDA botanist, and Elizabeth White, a farmer's daughter turned agricultural researcher, that our modern cultivated highbush blueberry was born in 1916. This mighty duo used grafts from exceptional wild plants growing along the cranberry bogs of Whitesbog, New Jersey, to breed our modern highbush cultivars. Due to the success of those cultivars, blueberries are now grown the world over.

An acre of blueberry bushes yields anywhere from 2,000 to 20,000 pounds of blueberries per year. Today there are four main types of blueberries grown throughout the United States:

- **Northern highbush** blueberry varieties grow best in the northern United States and Canada.

- **Southern highbush** varieties grow in Tennessee, Kentucky, Virginia, North Carolina, and along parts of the West Coast.

- **Rabbiteyes** grow in the southeastern United States and the Southern Hemisphere.

- **Lowbush,** the intensely flavored wild berry beloved in Maine, grows in New England and Canada.

These little jewels are prized for their sweet and tangy taste as well as their nutrition. Blueberries contain antioxidants (such as anthocyanin, which gives the berries their beautiful hue) and phytonutrients, both of which have powerful health benefits. These include the ability to reduce signs of aging, assist in controlling blood pressure and diabetes, and possibly improve heart health and lower the risk of cancer. Considered a superfood by many, blueberries can also help improve brain health, promote weight loss, and soothe inflammation. They pack a nutritional punch at only 80 calories per cup and boast vitamin C, iron, and fiber. Now that's a superfruit!

Unless otherwise noted, you can use fresh or frozen, wild or cultivated blueberries for the recipes in this book. When using frozen berries, there's no need to thaw them first, unless the recipe specifically says to do so. Although the recipes don't specify, wash your berries just before using.

Tips for Cooking with Blueberries

When purchasing fresh blueberries, choose berries that are plump and free from moisture and in clean, unstained containers. The dusty white coating on the berries is a natural substance and protects the berries from insects and bacteria.

Pick blueberries early in the day, as the fields heat up quickly and young children won't have the patience for picking in the hot sun. Pick only the ripe berries — they'll be a deep blue and separate easily from the stem — and leave the green ones to ripen another day. Use small containers, as the berries crush easily under too much weight from a deep container filled with berries. Chill the berries as soon as possible. A morning spent blueberry picking with the family at a local U-pick farm not only yields the freshest berries for your recipes, it creates fond memories that last a lifetime.

Blueberries should be stored unwashed and only washed immediately before use. Fresh berries keep refrigerated for just a few days, so use them up quickly or freeze.

Frozen blueberries, and particularly the antioxidant-rich wild blueberries, are widely available in 3-pound bags, making them ideal for keeping on hand year-round.

To freeze fresh berries, spread them out on a baking sheet, unwashed, and freeze. When frozen solid, pick out any extraneous plant material like stems or leaves and move the berries to freezer bags. I like to freeze them in 1-cup portions for easy use in recipes. Rinse quickly before using. Frozen blueberries will bring delight on a cold winter morning when added to buttermilk pancakes (see page 16).

You can substitute frozen berries for fresh in nearly every recipe. When using frozen berries, there's no need to thaw them first, unless the recipe specifically says to do so.

To boost blueberry flavor, mix in some wild blueberries with cultivated ones in most recipes. I take one-quarter of the volume required when using cultivated blueberries and substitute with frozen wild blueberries.

Blueberries are easily substituted for other summer fruit in your favorite recipes for cobblers, crisps, and most other sweet treats.

Dried blueberries are well suited to recipes where extra moisture would affect the texture of the finished product.

To dry your own blueberries, begin by plunging the washed berries in a mesh sieve or small-holed colander into boiling water for 30 seconds to crack their skins. Remove and dry thoroughly. Spread the blueberries in a single layer on a baking sheet and place in a preheated 175°F (80°C) oven. Stir the berries about once an hour. Depending on the moisture level of your berries, it can take up to 8 hours for the berries to shrivel and dry. Transfer the dried berries to a plastic bag or plastic container and store in an area away from sunlight. Watch for signs of condensation, which can encourage mold. If condensation occurs, redry the berries for another couple of hours.

The old adage of tossing blueberries in flour to prevent them from sinking in baked goods is ineffective, according to my recipe tests and the tests of many others. Toss if that's the way you were raised, but don't feel guilty if you don't.

Cook's Notes

INGREDIENTS

Quality ingredients yield quality results, so purchase the best-quality ingredients your food budget allows. Several baking recipes call for certain ingredients to be at room temperature. This provides for the best texture in cakes and muffins, and it also allows for some ingredients to be more easily integrated with others.

Baking powder and soda. Fresh (less than 1 year old) baking powder and baking soda are essential to baking success.

Butter. Unless otherwise specified, butter used in these recipes may be unsalted or salted.

Cream and milk. Heavy whipping cream is cream with at least 36 percent butterfat and is the best choice for rich, thick, billowy tufts of cream to be folded into dessert recipes or dolloped atop individual servings. Recipes calling for whole milk are best made with whole milk. Recipes not specifying can be made with any milk on hand.

Eggs. Large eggs are the standard for these recipes.

Lemon juice. Freshly squeezed lemon juice is preferred in recipes where the juice isn't heated during cooking, or in recipes where lemon is a dominant flavor (such as Blueberry-Lavender Lemonade, page 12).

Self-rising flour. For recipes calling for self-rising flour, you may substitute 1 cup all-purpose flour mixed with 1½ teaspoons baking powder and ¼ teaspoon salt. Flour is best stored in an airtight container and can remain fresh for up to 1 year if stored this way in a dry cabinet. Storing flour in the freezer extends the freshness up to 2 years.

Spices. For maximum flavor, restock spices that are more than 1 year old.

Vanilla extract. Use pure or imitation as your preference dictates. A well-respected food magazine conducted a blind taste test in which the participants preferred imitation vanilla for its simple vanilla taste. Suit your own taste buds.

METHODS

Whisk dry ingredients together for at least 30 seconds to ensure all of them are fully incorporated into the recipe. This is essential when making recipes that include baking powder, baking soda, or salt.

To measure flour by the cup, lightly whisk the flour in its container, then scoop spoonfuls of flour into a dry measuring cup and level it off with the back of a knife. If you are using a scale, 120 grams of flour equals 1 cup.

EQUIPMENT

Baking pans. Glass pie pans produce the crispiest crusts. Follow the visual cues for doneness as you get to know any new equipment.

Oven. Temperatures vary widely among ovens, and ovens often have hot spots. To identify hot spots in your oven, line a baking sheet with slices of store-bought white bread and bake the slices at 350°F (180°C). As the bread is toasting, you'll be able to identify the oven's hot spots by noticing which slices brown more quickly. Purchase an oven thermometer, an inexpensive insurance policy, to know how far off your oven temperature may be and compensate accordingly. You can also improve results for most baked goods by turning them 180 degrees from front to back halfway through the baking time.

Instant-read thermometer. Use this kitchen essential to determine if ingredients have been cooked to a proper temperature under food safety guidelines. It's another inexpensive tool to enhance your cooking.

Electric hand mixer. The time cues in the recipes that follow are written with these mixers in mind. If you are using a stand mixer, use the whisk attachment for egg whites and whipping cream, and the paddle attachment for all other ingredients. Watch for the visual cues for doneness as described in the recipes, knowing that a stand mixer will produce results more quickly than a hand mixer.

Blueberry Coffee Cake

(a.k.a. Crumb Cake)

MAKES ONE 9-INCH
SQUARE CAKE

Topping

- ¾ cup all-purpose flour
- ⅓ cup granulated sugar
- ⅓ cup firmly packed light brown sugar
- 1 teaspoon ground cinnamon
- Pinch of ground nutmeg
- Pinch of salt
- ⅓ cup unsalted butter, melted

Cake

- ⅓ cup butter, at room temperature
- ⅔ cup granulated sugar
- 2 eggs, at room temperature
- 1 teaspoon vanilla extract
- 1½ cups all-purpose flour
- 1 tablespoon baking powder
- ½ teaspoon salt
- ⅔ cup milk, at room temperature
- 1 cup fresh or frozen blueberries

Stacked high with crumble topping, this coffee cake rivals any you'd order in a bakery. The name crumb cake *must have been changed to* coffee cake *so we wouldn't feel guilty eating cake for breakfast. The room-temperature ingredients make for a light and fine-textured cake.*

MAKE THE TOPPING

1. Whisk together the flour, sugars, cinnamon, nutmeg, and salt in a small bowl until thoroughly combined, at least 30 seconds. Pour the melted butter over the flour mixture and work the butter into the mixture using your fingers or a fork until completely mixed. Set aside.

MAKE THE CAKE

2. Preheat the oven to 375°F (190°C). Spray or grease and flour a 9-inch square baking pan.

3. Beat the butter and sugar together in a large bowl with an electric hand mixer until light in color and fluffy, about 4 minutes. Beat in the eggs and vanilla until combined.

4. Whisk together the flour, baking powder, and salt in a medium bowl until thoroughly combined, at least 30 seconds. Add the dry ingredients to the butter mixture in thirds, alternating with half the milk, beating until combined and scraping the bottom of the bowl between each addition. Gently fold in the blueberries.

5. Transfer the batter to the prepared pan, leveling with a spatula, and sprinkle evenly with the crumble topping. Bake for 35 to 40 minutes, or until a toothpick inserted into the center comes out clean (avoiding a blueberry). Cool for 10 minutes in the pan before cutting. Serve warm.

1954 Blueberry "Boy-Bait"

MAKES ONE 9- BY 13-INCH CAKE

---

2 cups all-purpose flour

1½ cups sugar

⅔ cup unsalted butter, cut into small pieces

2 teaspoons baking powder

1 teaspoon salt

2 egg yolks

1 cup milk

2 egg whites

1 cup fresh or frozen blueberries

½ cup confectioners' sugar

This award-winning recipe, complete with its name, comes from Renny Powell, who, at the age of 15, won second place in the Junior Contest at the 1954 Pillsbury's Grand National Recipe and Baking Contest held at the Waldorf-Astoria Hotel in New York City. She knew this coffee cake would change her social life and named it accordingly! It could change yours, too. Let's call it Date-Bait in this new millennium. This recipe is her original.

1. Preheat the oven to 350°F (180°C). Spray or grease and flour a 9- by 13-inch baking pan.

2. Whisk together the flour and sugar in a large bowl until thoroughly combined, at least 30 seconds. Cut in the butter with a pastry blender, two knives, or two forks, until the mixture becomes fine crumbs. Set aside ½ cup of the mixture for the topping.

3. Add the baking powder, salt, egg yolks, and milk to the flour mixture and beat with an electric hand mixer for 3 minutes. Clean the beaters.

4. Place the egg whites in a separate bowl and beat until stiff peaks form, 4 to 5 minutes. Fold gently into the batter and spread the batter in the prepared pan. Arrange the blueberries over the batter and sprinkle with the reserved flour-and-sugar topping.

5. Bake for 35 to 40 minutes, or until golden brown and a toothpick inserted in the center comes out clean (avoiding a blueberry). Transfer to a wire rack to cool. Dust with confectioners' sugar sprinkled through a fine mesh sieve. Cut into squares and serve warm.

Dried Blueberry–Orange Scones

MAKES 8 SCONES

- ¼ cup granulated sugar
- Zest of 2 oranges
- 2 cups all-purpose flour, plus more for shaping the dough
- 1 tablespoon baking powder
- ½ teaspoon salt
- ½ cup (1 stick) unsalted butter, cut into ½-inch pieces
- ¾ cup dried wild blueberries
- 2 eggs
- ¾ cup heavy cream
- ½ teaspoon vanilla extract
- 1 egg white
- 2 tablespoons water
- Decorating sugar or other large-grain sugar

Scones are an almost-biscuit, only a little denser and drier, plus scones use an egg as binding. I find these scones hit the mark — not a biscuit, but delicious.

1. Line a baking sheet with parchment paper.

2. Use your fingers to rub the granulated sugar and orange zest together in a small bowl until thoroughly combined. Place the orange-sugar mixture, flour, baking powder, and salt in a food processor fitted with a metal blade. Pulse three or four times to combine. Scatter the butter pieces over the flour. Pulse until the butter is the size of small peas, about five times. Transfer to a large bowl. Scatter the dried blueberries over the mixture and toss lightly to mix.

3. Lightly whisk together the eggs, cream, and vanilla in a small bowl.

4. Make a well in the center of the flour mixture using the back of your hand. Pour the cream mixture into the well. Using broad strokes, stir together the cream and flour with a silicone spatula until the batter just comes together in a single mass.

5. Turn out the dough onto a floured work surface and lightly knead and press the dough together, three or four strokes, until it is a cohesive dough. Press and shape the dough into an 8- to 9-inch-wide circle no more than ¾ inch thick.

6. Cut the dough in half with a sharp knife and continue cutting until you have eight equal pie-shaped pieces. Transfer the pieces to the prepared baking sheet, reassembling them in a round, but leaving ½ inch between the slices.

7. Whisk the egg white and water together in a small bowl and brush on the scones. Move the scones to the refrigerator for 30 minutes to set the dough. Preheat the oven to 400°F (200°F).

8. Remove the baking sheet from the refrigerator, sprinkle the scones with decorating sugar, and bake for about 35 minutes, or until browned and a toothpick inserted in the center comes out clean (avoiding a blueberry). Cool slightly and transfer from the baking sheet to a wire rack to cool completely, or serve warm.

Rachel's Blueberry-Matcha Smoothie

MAKES ONE 10-OUNCE
SERVING

1 cup yogurt

½ cup unsweetened vanilla
almond milk

⅓ cup frozen blueberries

1½ teaspoons matcha powder

8 whole almonds

1 teaspoon honey

Mix and match and make your own creation. Full-fat, low-fat, and nonfat yogurt, plain or flavored, are all welcome options in this recipe. Bump up the amount of matcha if you are a big fan. I love to use a bit of wild blueberry honey in this recipe.

Combine the yogurt, almond milk, blueberries, matcha, almonds, and honey in a blender or food processor and process for at least 30 seconds to pulverize almonds. Serve immediately.

Blueberry-Lavender Lemonade

MAKES EIGHT 8-OUNCE
SERVINGS

2 cups fresh or frozen
blueberries

½ cup sugar, plus more as
needed

2 tablespoons dried lavender
flowers

1 cup water, plus more as
needed

2 cups ice, plus more for
serving

½ cup freshly squeezed
lemon juice

1 lemon, sliced, for garnish
(optional)

Bright, beautiful, and refreshing, this pale magenta refresher is a must for a summer party or family gathering. Culinary lavender flowers are found in the spice aisle of the grocery store and are a fabulous addition to beverages.

1. Combine the blueberries, sugar, lavender, and water in a medium saucepan over high heat and bring to a boil. Boil for about 5 minutes. Remove from the heat and let cool for 15 minutes.

2. Place the ice in a half-gallon pitcher or container. Set a strainer over the pitcher and strain the blueberry mixture over the ice, pressing down on the blueberries to extract all their juice. Discard the solids, or reserve them to make No-Waste Blueberry Butter (page 26).

3. Add the lemon juice to the pitcher and stir. Add additional cold water and sugar to taste as needed to reach the desired concentration and flavor. To serve, pour the lemonade over glasses filled with ice and garnish with lemon slices, if desired.

Make-Ahead Blueberry-Pecan French Toast Casserole

MAKES 6 SERVINGS

1 large loaf French bread, cut into 1-inch-thick slices

6 eggs

2 cups whole milk

1 teaspoon vanilla extract

½ teaspoon ground nutmeg

½ teaspoon salt

1 cup firmly packed light or dark brown sugar

4 tablespoons unsalted butter

2 cups fresh or frozen wild blueberries

1 cup chopped pecans

Maple syrup, for serving (optional)

Overnight guests will adore waking up to this warm, nutty French toast casserole — and it's easy on the cook. Assemble this dish the night before to allow the bread to fully absorb the egg mixture.

1. Rub the inside of a 9- by 13-inch casserole dish with a little butter and arrange the bread slices in a single layer in the dish.

2. Whisk together the eggs, milk, vanilla, nutmeg, salt, and ¼ cup of the sugar in a medium bowl. Pour the mixture evenly over the bread slices. Cover and refrigerate the casserole overnight, or for at least 8 hours.

3. When ready to bake, preheat the oven to 400°F (200°C). While the oven is heating, remove the casserole from the refrigerator.

4. Melt the butter and the remaining ¾ cup sugar in a small saucepan over medium heat, stirring well to mix.

5. Evenly toss the blueberries and pecans over the casserole. Drizzle the warm sugar mixture over the top and bake the casserole for 45 to 50 minutes, or until set and golden brown on top.

6. Serve with maple syrup, if desired.

Buttermilk Blueberry Pancakes
with Blueberry Maple Syrup

MAKES ABOUT EIGHT 4-INCH
PANCAKES

Syrup

1 cup fresh blueberries

1 cup maple syrup

Pancakes

1 cup all-purpose flour

2 teaspoons baking powder

2 tablespoons sugar

½ teaspoon salt

1 egg

1 cup buttermilk

3 tablespoons butter, melted

1 cup fresh blueberries

Flapjacks, griddle cakes, or pancakes — they all mean a warm breakfast treat slathered with butter and topped with syrup. By waiting to add the blueberries until the first side is cooking, you reduce the chances of the batter turning blue. This recipe doubles easily for a crowd.

MAKE THE SYRUP

1. Heat the blueberries and maple syrup in a small saucepan over medium heat and cook for 3 to 4 minutes. Smash the berries with a potato masher or other implement, and cook for 2 minutes longer. Stir and remove from the heat.

MAKE THE PANCAKES

2. Preheat the oven to 200°F (95°C).

3. Whisk together the flour, baking powder, sugar, and salt in a large bowl until thoroughly combined, at least 30 seconds.

4. Beat the egg, buttermilk, and butter together in a medium-size deep bowl with an electric hand mixer until light, about 2 minutes. Pour the egg mixture into the flour mixture and beat just until combined.

5. When ready to cook, heat a large skillet over medium-low heat. The skillet is ready when a few water droplets scattered on the hot surface dance and evaporate quickly.

6. For each pancake, use about ¼ cup batter. Sprinkle blueberries on top as the first side cooks. Cook the first side until bubbles form on the surface and the edges start to look dry, about 3 minutes. Turn the pancakes, then continue cooking until nicely browned on the underside, about 2 minutes. Move to a platter and transfer to the preheated oven to keep warm while cooking the remaining pancakes. Serve warm with butter and blueberry maple syrup.

Blueberry Cinnamon-Spiced Doughnuts
with Vanilla Glaze

MAKES 6 DOUGHNUTS

Doughnuts

¼ cup granulated sugar

   Zest of 1 orange

¾ cup all-purpose flour

½ teaspoon baking powder

¼ teaspoon baking soda

¼ teaspoon ground cinnamon

¼ teaspoon salt

1 egg

½ cup plain Greek yogurt

2 tablespoons milk

2 tablespoons canola oil or other neutral oil

¾ cup fresh blueberries

Glaze

1 cup confectioners' sugar, sifted

2 tablespoons light corn syrup

1–2 tablespoons milk

½ teaspoon vanilla extract

You can have fresh, hot doughnuts any time! These spiced doughnuts will rival any bakery doughnut. The corn syrup in the glaze stabilizes the sugar mixture, making it more opaque and longer lasting.

MAKE THE DOUGHNUTS

1. Preheat the oven to 350°F (180°C). Spray or grease and flour a six-portion doughnut pan.

2. Use your fingers to rub the granulated sugar and orange zest together in a large bowl until the zest is fully incorporated. Whisk in the flour, baking powder, baking soda, cinnamon, and salt until thoroughly combined, at least 30 seconds.

3. Whisk together the egg, yogurt, milk, and oil in a small bowl. Stir the egg mixture into the flour mixture until just combined. Gently fold in the blueberries.

4. Transfer the mixture to a piping bag or a plastic bag and snip off the end of the plastic bag. Pipe the batter into the doughnut pan molds.

5. Bake the doughnuts for 22 to 25 minutes, or until golden brown and a toothpick inserted in the center comes out clean (avoiding a blueberry). Let the pan cool for 5 minutes. Using a small offset spatula if necessary, gingerly remove the doughnuts from the pan to a wire rack to cool.

MAKE THE GLAZE

6. While the doughnuts are cooling, stir together the confectioners' sugar, corn syrup, milk, and vanilla in a small bowl until thoroughly combined. Dip one side of each cooled doughnut into the glaze and return to the rack. Serve immediately.

Jumbo Bakery-Style Ginger-Blueberry Muffins

MAKES 6 JUMBO MUFFINS

- 3 cups all-purpose flour
- 4 teaspoons baking powder
- 1 teaspoon ground cinnamon
- ½ teaspoon salt
- 1 cup granulated sugar
- 2 eggs
- 1 cup milk
- ½ cup canola oil or other neutral oil
- 1 teaspoon vanilla extract
- ½ teaspoon almond extract
- 2 cups fresh or frozen blueberries
- ¼ cup finely chopped crystallized ginger
- Decorating sugar or other large-grain sugar

These fluffy, big bakery-style muffins have it all — taste, texture, and eye appeal — and were awarded a blue ribbon in the Machias Wild Blueberry Festival in Maine in 2019. A light zing of ginger, a little zip of spice, and the crunch from the topping of coarse sugar fit the bill. If the muffins aren't devoured in one sitting, slice one open, toast, and slather with butter for a treat later. These muffins are best made with fresh blueberries.

1. Set an oven rack in the center of the oven. Preheat the oven to 425°F (220°C). Spray a jumbo six-muffin pan with cooking spray or coat lightly with oil.

2. Whisk together the flour, baking powder, cinnamon, and salt in a large bowl. Add the granulated sugar and whisk until thoroughly combined, at least 30 seconds.

3. Break up the eggs in a medium bowl with a whisk and whisk in the milk, oil, vanilla, and almond extract.

4. Make a well in the flour mixture and pour the egg mixture into the well. Using a silicone spatula, fold the egg mixture into the flour, scraping the bottom of the bowl at each turn. Mix gently but quickly. Avoid overmixing the batter.

5. Toss the blueberries and ginger on top of the batter and fold gently to incorporate the berries. Spoon the batter into the prepared muffin pan, filling each cup to the rim. Sprinkle the tops with decorating sugar.

6. Bake for 5 minutes. Reduce the oven temperature to 375°F (190°C) and bake for 25 to 26 minutes longer, or until tops are light golden and a toothpick inserted in the center comes out clean (avoiding a blueberry). Let cool for 10 minutes in the pan. Serve warm, or transfer to a wire rack to cool for storing. These muffins freeze well.

Make-Ahead Blueberry Jam Breakfast Danishes

MAKES TWO 4½- BY 12-INCH
DANISHES

Danishes

1 box puff pastry sheets

4 ounces cream cheese, at
room temperature

¼ cup granulated sugar

½ teaspoon vanilla extract

½ cup Small-Batch Easy
Refrigerator Blueberry Jam
or Blueberry-Lime Jam
(page 28)

1 egg

1 tablespoon water

Decorating sugar or
other large-grain sugar

Glaze

½ cup confectioners' sugar

1–2 tablespoons milk or cream

½ teaspoon vanilla extract

Easy and elegant, these Danishes can be assembled in advance, frozen, and baked whenever the mood strikes, making them a stress-free breakfast treat — especially for overnight guests.

MAKE THE DANISHES

1. Thaw the puff pastry according to package directions. Line a baking sheet with parchment paper.

2. Stir together the cream cheese, granulated sugar, and vanilla in a small bowl.

3. Roll out each pastry sheet to 9 by 12 inches. Cut each sheet in half lengthwise to form four pieces 4½ inches wide and 12 inches long. Move two pieces to the prepared baking sheet.

4. Using an offset spatula, divide the cream cheese mixture equally between the two pieces on the baking sheet and spread over each of the two rectangles, leaving a ½-inch border on all sides.

5. Stir the blueberry jam and add a few drops of water, if necessary, to make it spreadable. Divide the jam equally between the two cream cheese–coated rectangles and slather directly on top of the cream cheese.

6. Whisk the egg with the water in a small bowl and lightly brush the egg wash along the ½-inch border of each rectangle, reserving some egg wash for the tops.

7. Using a sharp knife, cut diagonal slits in the remaining two rectangles, leaving a ½-inch border. Place each rectangle on one of the cream cheese and jam–covered rectangles on the baking sheet.

8. Seal the edges of each rectangle together by crimping with the tines of a fork. Brush the remaining egg wash over the tops. Sprinkle with decorating sugar.

9. Move the baking sheet to the refrigerator and chill 30 minutes, or freeze the Danishes overnight.

10. When ready to bake, preheat the oven to 375°F (190°C).

11. When the oven is hot, move the baking sheet from the refrigerator or freezer to the oven and bake for 20 to 25 minutes for refrigerated Danishes, or about 30 minutes for frozen, until puffy and golden brown.

MAKE THE GLAZE

12. While the pastries are baking, mix together the confectioners' sugar, milk, and vanilla in a small bowl. Drizzle over the warm Danishes and serve.

No-Waste Blueberry Butter

MAKES 6 HALF-PINT JARS

5½ cups blueberry pulp

3 cups sugar, plus more as needed

1 tablespoon lemon zest

1½ tablespoons freshly squeezed lemon juice

¼ teaspoon ground nutmeg

Feel virtuous about your kitchen scraps and make them into this luscious spread that glides beautifully on toast, English muffins, or bagels. Just like an apple butter recipe, this blueberry butter doesn't call for any butter. Use any discarded blueberry pulp for this recipe, such as that from Blueberry Simple Syrup (page 54), Blueberry-Lavender Lemonade (page 12), Blueberry Shrub (page 40), or Homemade Blueberry Vodka (page 67). Adjust the amount of sugar based on the taste of the pulp used.

1. Purée the blueberry pulp in a food processor until very smooth, about 1 minute.

2. Stir together the processed pulp, sugar, lemon zest, lemon juice, and nutmeg in a large pot. Bring to a boil over medium heat, stirring often. Reduce the heat and add additional sugar to taste, if needed. Simmer until the mixture thickens and holds its shape on a spoon, about 1 hour. Stir often, scraping the bottom of the pot, to prevent burning.

3. The blueberry butter can be refrigerated for up to 4 weeks, frozen for up to 6 months, or canned using appropriate canning methods and stored for up to 1 year.

Small-Batch Easy
Refrigerator Blueberry Jam

MAKES 2 HALF-PINT JARS

- 2 cups fresh or frozen blueberries
- ¾ cup sugar
- 2 teaspoons lemon juice
- Pinch of ground cinnamon

Refrigerator jam brings all the joys of nature's seasonal bounty inside, without the need for traditional canning. This jam is not safe for long-term storage, so enjoy it within about 3 to 4 weeks. It may be frozen in a freezer-safe container for 6 months.

Combine 1 cup of the blueberries, the sugar, lemon juice, and cinnamon in a medium saucepan over medium heat. Cook until the berries are bubbling and have begun to soften, 5 to 8 minutes, then add the remaining 1 cup blueberries. Reduce the heat to low and continue cooking until all the berries are soft and a spoon leaves a line of separation in the jam when scraping the bottom of the pan, about 25 minutes. Cool and fill clean glass jars or freezer-safe containers.

Blueberry-Lime Jam

**MAKES 5 HALF-PINT JARS
(ABOUT 5 CUPS)**

- 4½ cups fresh or frozen wild Maine blueberries
- 6 tablespoons classic pectin (I use Ball brand)
- 5 cups sugar
- 1 tablespoon lime zest
- ⅓ cup freshly squeezed lime juice

This classic jam is one worth canning for your pantry, as cold, dark winter mornings are much brighter when homemade blueberry jam appears. Canning is easy and fun, but always follow proper canning procedures to ensure safety. When in doubt, consult your local extension service or an online canning supply manufacturer. Have all the equipment ready before beginning.

1. To prepare the jars, cover a kitchen counter with a large clean towel. Place a rack in the bottom of a large deep pot with a lid. Add the empty half-pint canning jars and fill the pot with water, covering the jars by 2 inches. Bring the water to a simmer. Leave the jars simmering until needed, adding additional water as needed to keep the volume 2 inches higher than the jars. Wash the canning rings

and new lids in hot soapy water and leave to dry on the towel. Dip a widemouthed funnel into the simmering water and remove to the towel.

2. While the jars are simmering, mash the blueberries using a potato masher or other implement, one layer at a time, in the bottom of a 2-quart saucepan. Stir in the pectin and bring to a boil over medium-high heat. Add the sugar and stir well until the sugar dissolves. Stir in the lime zest and lime juice. Bring to a steady boil (this can take 3 to 5 minutes) and boil hard for 1 minute, stirring constantly and scraping the bottom of the pot.

3. Using canning tongs, transfer the jars to the towel. Place the widemouthed funnel into the first jar and carefully ladle hot jam into the jar, leaving ¼ inch of headspace. Fill the remaining jars. Using standard tongs, dip part of a folded paper towel in the boiling water and wipe the jar rims free of any drips.

4. Top the jars with lids and rings, tightening the rings with just fingertip strength.

5. Using canning tongs, return the filled jars to the pot of simmering water, making sure that the jars are covered by 2 inches of water, and increase the heat to high. When the water is boiling, cover the pot and boil the filled jars for 10 minutes. Remove the pot from the heat, uncover, and let sit for 5 minutes before using canning tongs to transfer the jars to the towel.

6. Allow the jars to sit undisturbed for 12 to 24 hours. Remove the rings and check the seals (the lids should be indented, with no leaks, and should not lift off the rim easily), then replace and tighten the rings. Any jars without a tight seal on the lid aren't safe for long-term storage but are delightful if refrigerated and consumed in less than 1 month.

Blueberry-Pecan Bread

MAKES ONE 9- BY 5-INCH LOAF

2½ cups all-purpose flour

¾ cup sugar

1 tablespoon baking powder

½ teaspoon salt

⅓ cup butter, cut into ½-inch cubes

¾ cup chopped pecans

2 eggs

1 cup milk

1 teaspoon vanilla extract

2 cups fresh or frozen blueberries

This bread is marvelous sliced, toasted, and slathered with butter. Select your favorite nut for this treat, such as pecans or walnuts. The recipe doubles easily, so make an extra as a gift.

1. Preheat the oven to 350°F (180°C). Spray or grease and flour a 9- by 5-inch loaf pan.

2. Whisk together the flour, sugar, baking powder, and salt in a large bowl until thoroughly combined, at least 30 seconds. Scatter the butter cubes over the flour mixture and the rub butter into the flour using your fingers, or cut the butter into the flour with a pastry blender, two knives, or two forks, until the mixture becomes fine crumbs. Toss ½ cup of the nuts into the flour mixture. Make a well in the center of the flour.

3. Whisk the eggs lightly in a medium bowl and whisk in the milk and vanilla. Pour the egg mixture into the well in the flour mixture and stir gently but thoroughly, scraping the bottom of the bowl, until the mixture is just combined. Avoid overmixing. Gently fold the blueberries into the batter.

4. Scoop the batter into the prepared pan and top with the remaining ¼ cup nuts. Bake for about 1 hour 10 minutes, or until a toothpick inserted in the center comes out clean (avoiding a blueberry).

5. Let the bread cool in the pan for 10 minutes. Run a knife around the edges of the pan to loosen the bread and transfer to a wire rack to cool.

Blueberry and Red Onion Salsa

MAKES 1 CUP

- 1 cup fresh blueberries
- 3 tablespoons minced red onion
- 2 tablespoons chopped fresh basil
- 2 teaspoons white balsamic vinegar
- Salt and freshly ground black pepper

Grab the chips and enjoy this special summertime salsa. Reserve a small basil leaf or two for garnishing the top of the salsa. Substitute white wine vinegar or another light vinegar if white balsamic is not available.

1. Smash half of the blueberries in the bottom of a small bowl with a potato masher or other implement.

2. Add the remaining blueberries, the onion, basil, and vinegar, and toss to combine. Season to taste with salt and pepper.

3. Refrigerate until serving. This may be made up to 8 hours in advance.

Buttermilk Blueberry Soup

MAKES 6 SERVINGS

2 cups fresh or frozen blueberries, plus more for garnish

½ cup water

½ cup sugar

½ teaspoon orange zest

2 tablespoons orange juice

2 cups buttermilk

Made with fresh blueberries and served cold in summer, this soup is a refreshing first course or a fine dessert, depending on the amount of sugar used. Finland, Norway, Sweden, and Poland all have variations of this fruit soup, some with gelatin or potato starch as thickeners.

1. Heat the blueberries, water, sugar, orange zest, and orange juice in a medium saucepan over medium-high heat and bring to a boil. Reduce the heat to low, cover, and simmer for 15 minutes.

2. Transfer the soup to a blender (or blend with an immersion blender) and purée until smooth. Stir in the buttermilk.

3. Chill the soup until cold, and serve garnished with blueberries.

Wild Blueberry, Horseradish, and Blue Cheese Spread

MAKES ABOUT 1 CUP

- 3 ounces blue cheese, at room temperature
- 4 ounces whipped cream cheese, at room temperature
- 1 teaspoon prepared grated white horseradish, plus more as needed
- 1 scallion, thinly sliced, both white and green parts
- ½ teaspoon salt, plus more as needed
- ½ teaspoon freshly ground black pepper, plus more as needed
- ¼ cup fresh or frozen wild blueberries
- 2 tablespoons finely chopped walnuts

This spread assembles easily, but it needs to chill for about an hour after mixing for maximum flavor. Bring the blue cheese and cream cheese to room temperature before you begin. This recipe doubles easily for a crowd. Serve with multigrain crackers.

1. Place the blue cheese in a medium mixing bowl and break up with a fork.

2. Add the cream cheese, horseradish, scallion, salt, and pepper, and stir to blend.

3. Add the blueberries and walnuts, and stir just until mixed in. Adjust the seasoning to taste, adding more horseradish if desired.

4. Refrigerate for at least 1 hour before serving.

Blueberry, Watermelon, Feta Cheese, and Mint Salad

MAKES 4 SERVINGS

- 1 teaspoon Dijon mustard
- 1 teaspoon honey
- 2 tablespoons red or white wine vinegar
- ½ cup extra-virgin olive oil
  Salt and freshly ground black pepper
- 2 cups watermelon, cut into ½-inch cubes
- 1 pint fresh blueberries
- 6 ounces feta cheese, crumbled or grated
  Chopped fresh herbs such as basil, thyme, or rosemary

This salad is summer in a bowl. The red, white, and blue combination brightens any summer meal. For a significant side dish, place this fruit salad on a bed of mixed greens.

1. Combine the mustard and honey in a small bowl. Whisk in the vinegar. While whisking, slowly drizzle in the oil and continue whisking until emulsified. Season to taste with salt and pepper.

2. Place the watermelon, blueberries, and cheese in a large bowl. Serve with the reserved dressing and top with fresh herbs to taste. If making ahead, dress just before serving.

Blueberry Shrub

4 cups fresh blueberries

2 cups apple cider vinegar

2 cups sugar

Ice cubes or crushed ice, for serving

Skewers of fresh blueberries, for garnish (optional)

A shrub is a vinegar-based fruit syrup used to make a thirst-quenching drink that is most popular in summer months. Brought from England by colonists, shrubs have a rich history in American cooking.

1. Place the blueberries in a large nonmetallic bowl or container. Add the vinegar, cover tightly, and refrigerate for at least 3 days.

2. Pour the vinegar-marinated blueberries into a sieve over a medium saucepan. Press down on the berries to release all their juice. Discard the solids, or reserve them to make No-Waste Blueberry Butter (page 26).

3. Stir the sugar into the juice and bring to a boil over high heat. Cook for 3 minutes, stirring occasionally. Remove from the heat and let cool. Pour the sweetened blueberry liquid into a container and chill.

4. To make each drink, add ¼ cup of the blueberry shrub concentrate to a medium glass filled with ice and add 1 cup cold water or sparkling water. Garnish with a berry skewer, if desired.

Spinach, Blood Orange, Goat Cheese, and Bacon Salad

with Blueberry Vinaigrette

MAKES 4 SERVINGS

Salad

- 8 ounces baby spinach leaves
- 1 avocado, cubed
- 1 blood orange, peel and white pith removed and sliced into wheels
- ¼ cup goat cheese crumbles
- 2 slices bacon, crisply fried and finely chopped

Vinaigrette

- 1 cup fresh or frozen blueberries
- ½ cup extra-virgin olive oil
- ¼ cup balsamic vinegar
- 2 tablespoons Dijon mustard
- Pinch of salt

This mix-and-match salad can be made your own by substituting any greens, citrus, or cheese according to your family's preference. The dressing can also be used on a fruit salad as a snappy contrast.

MAKE THE SALAD

1. Divide the spinach equally among four plates. Place one-quarter of the remaining ingredients onto each plate in the following order: avocado, orange, cheese, bacon.

MAKE THE VINAIGRETTE

2. Place the blueberries, oil, vinegar, mustard, and salt in a blender or food processor and blend until smooth. Drizzle on top of the salads just before serving. Store the remaining dressing in a glass jar. Shake well before using.

Gluten-Free Blueberry Buttermilk Corn Muffins

MAKES 12 MUFFINS

1¾ cups gluten-free flour

1 cup yellow cornmeal

⅓ cup sugar

1 tablespoon baking powder

½ teaspoon salt

1¼ cups buttermilk

2 eggs

½ cup (1 stick) unsalted butter, at room temperature

1 cup fresh or frozen blueberries

Much less sweet than regular blueberry muffins, these corn muffins are great for a snack or even a light dessert. Serve warm, or cool and wrap to store in the refrigerator or freezer. Rewarm in a 350°F (180°C) oven.

1. Set an oven rack in the center of the oven. Preheat the oven to 400°F (200°C). Line a standard 12-cup muffin pan with paper liners. Alternatively, spray or grease and flour the muffin cups.

2. Whisk together the flour, cornmeal, sugar, baking powder, and salt in a large deep bowl until thoroughly combined, at least 30 seconds.

3. Add the buttermilk, eggs, and butter to the flour. Beat together with an electric hand mixer on high speed for about 2 minutes. The batter will be very thick.

4. Divide the batter equally among the muffin cups. Scatter the blueberries on top of the muffins and lightly tap the berries with the tip of a dull knife to submerge or partially submerge the berries.

5. Bake for 22 to 25 minutes, or until the muffins are cooked through and a toothpick inserted in the center comes out clean (avoiding a blueberry). Let the muffins cool for 5 to 10 minutes before removing from the pan. Serve warm, or transfer the muffins to a wire rack to cool completely before storing.

Warm Grilled Chicken and Blueberry Salad

MAKES 4 SERVINGS

- 1 pound chicken breasts
- 2 teaspoons salt, plus more as needed
- 1 teaspoon freshly ground black pepper, plus more as needed
- 1 tablespoon extra-virgin olive oil
- ½ cup plain Greek yogurt
- 1 teaspoon lemon zest
- 1 tablespoon freshly squeezed lemon juice
- 1 teaspoon garlic powder
- 1 cup fresh blueberries
- ¾ cup chopped celery (about 3 stalks)
- ¼ red onion, finely chopped
- ¼ cup parsley, chopped

Bright tangy flavors, crunchy textured vegetables, and moist grilled chicken make for a satisfying meal. Serve alone in a bowl, on a bed of greens, or in a sandwich.

1. Heat a grill pan over medium-high heat. Season the chicken with the salt and pepper. If the chicken breasts are particularly large, cut them in half horizontally before cooking. Coat the hot grill pan with the oil and sear the chicken for 5 to 6 minutes on each side or until the internal temperature reaches 165°F (74°C) on an instant-read thermometer. Remove to a chopping board. When cooled slightly, chop the chicken and transfer to a large bowl.

2. Stir together the yogurt, lemon zest, lemon juice, and garlic powder in a small bowl.

3. Add the blueberries, celery, onion, and yogurt mixture to the chicken and toss to coat. Season to taste with additional salt and pepper. Serve the salad in bowls, sprinkled with the parsley.

Salmon Fillets
with Blueberry-Onion Jam Glaze

MAKES 4–6 SERVINGS

Jam

- 1 tablespoon extra-virgin olive oil
- 2 onions, sliced
- 1 cup fresh or frozen blueberries
- 1 cup water
- ¼ cup balsamic vinegar
- 1–2 tablespoons firmly packed brown sugar
- Salt and freshly ground black pepper

Salmon

- 4–6 salmon steaks or fillets
- Salt and freshly ground pepper
- Fresh basil leaves, for garnish (optional)

Salmon is a year-round favorite, and blueberries love vinegar and onions, making a savory topping for the fish. Double the jam ingredients and use extra with any leftovers as an innovative sandwich spread (see page 58).

MAKE THE JAM

1. Heat a large skillet over medium heat. When hot, add the oil and onions and cook for 2 minutes. Reduce the heat to low and cook until the onions are wilted and starting to turn brown, about 20 minutes, stirring occasionally.

2. Stir in the blueberries, water, and vinegar. Increase the heat to medium and cook until the blueberries have softened, about 5 minutes. Season with the sugar and salt and pepper to taste. Set aside.

COOK THE SALMON

3. Preheat the oven to 400°F (200°C). Line a baking sheet with foil. Place the salmon fillets on the sheet and season with salt and pepper.

4. Bake for 12 to 15 minutes, depending on the thickness of the salmon (about 10 minutes per inch of thickness), until the salmon is still slightly pink in the center. Remove the baking sheet from the oven, and spoon a portion of the jam glaze over each fillet. Garnish with basil leaves, if desired, and serve hot.

Sautéed Pork Tenderloin
with Blueberry Balsamic Mustard Glaze

MAKES 3–4 SERVINGS

Glaze

- 2 cups fresh or frozen blueberries
- ½ cup balsamic vinegar
- 1 tablespoon maple syrup
- 1½ tablespoons whole-grain mustard
- Pinch of salt
- Pinch of freshly ground black pepper

Pork

- 1 (1-pound) pork tenderloin
- Salt and freshly ground black pepper
- 1 teaspoon extra-virgin olive oil
- Fresh sage leaves, for garnish (optional)

Whether sliced and sautéed or baked whole in the oven, pork tenderloins are a quick-cooking main course. Add colorful side dishes like sweet potatoes and broccoli.

MAKE THE GLAZE

1. Combine 1 cup of the blueberries with the vinegar in a small saucepan and bring to a quick boil over medium-high heat. Mash the blueberries with a potato masher or other implement, then add the remaining 1 cup blueberries. Reduce the heat to low and cook, stirring occasionally, until the glaze is thickened and reduced in volume by half. Stir in the maple syrup, mustard, salt, and pepper. Keep warm.

COOK THE TENDERLOIN ON THE STOVETOP

2. Slice the tenderloin into 1-inch-thick medallions (rounds). Season with salt and pepper.

3. Heat a large skillet over medium-high heat. When hot, add the oil. Add the medallions in a single layer and sear, cooking for about 3 minutes. Turn and cook for 3 minutes longer. Pour ½ cup of the glaze into the skillet and turn the medallions over in the skillet until coated. Remove from the heat and garnish with sage leaves, if desired. Serve warm and pass extra glaze.

BAKE THE TENDERLOIN IN THE OVEN

4. Preheat the oven to 400°F (200°C). Line a baking sheet with foil.

5. Place the tenderloin on the prepared baking sheet and season with salt and pepper. Roast for 20 to 30 minutes, or until the internal temperature of the thickest part of the meat registers 150°F (65°C) on an instant-read thermometer. Transfer to a carving board to rest for 5 minutes.

6. Carve, then move the carved slices to a skillet over medium heat and toss with half of the glaze. Garnish with sage leaves, if desired. Serve warm and pass extra glaze.

Whole Roast Chicken
with Blueberry Chutney

Chicken

1 (3½-pound) whole chicken

3 tablespoons butter, at room temperature

Salt and freshly ground black pepper

1 lemon

1–2 sprigs rosemary

Chutney

2 medium shallots, finely chopped

½ cup apple cider vinegar

⅓ cup firmly packed light or dark brown sugar

4 cups fresh blueberries

¼ cup chopped crystallized ginger

Zest and juice of 2 lemons

¼ teaspoon ground cinnamon

¼ teaspoon red pepper flakes

Simple roast chicken gets a lift from this tangy-sweet chutney. It's a taste reminiscent of cranberry sauce, fresh and fruity with a slight bite.

ROAST THE CHICKEN

1. Preheat the oven to 400°F (200°C).

2. Rub the skin of the entire bird with the butter and season with salt and pepper. Cut both ends off the lemon, then cut the lemon in half. Insert the lemon halves and rosemary into the cavity of the chicken and transfer the chicken to a roasting pan.

3. Roast the chicken in the oven for about 1 hour, or until the temperature of the thickest part of the thigh reaches 175°F (80°C) on an instant-read thermometer. Transfer the chicken to a cutting board and allow it to rest for 10 to 15 minutes, then carve and serve with chutney.

MAKE THE CHUTNEY

4. While the chicken is roasting, combine the shallots, vinegar, and sugar in a skillet. Bring to a boil over medium-high heat, then reduce the heat to low and simmer until the liquid is reduced by half. Stir in the blueberries, ginger, lemon zest and juice, cinnamon, and pepper flakes, and cook until the excess juices begin to evaporate, 5 to 10 minutes. Remove the skillet from the heat and let the chutney sit until serving.

Blueberry, Bourbon, and Mint Muddle

MAKES 1 COCKTAIL

¼ cup fresh or frozen blueberries, plus 6 blueberries for garnish

8 fresh mint leaves, plus more for garnish

1 teaspoon lemon juice

1 tablespoon Blueberry Simple Syrup (see below)

2 ounces bourbon

2–3 drops Angostura bitters

Ice cubes or crushed ice

Club soda

Bourbon and other brown liquors are thought to be cold-weather drinks, but this bourbon muddle — with its cool hit of mint, bright lemon juice, and light bubbles of club soda — is just right for summer. Substitute maple syrup for the simple syrup if you have the real thing on hand. When using frozen blueberries, allow them to thaw before using.

Muddle the blueberries in the bottom of a cocktail shaker. Add the mint leaves and muddle lightly, just until the leaves are bruised but not ground up. Add the lemon juice, syrup, bourbon, and bitters. Shake well to combine. Pour the mixture over ice in a rocks glass and top with club soda. Garnish with the extra mint leaves and blueberries.

Blueberry Simple Syrup

MAKES ABOUT 1¼ CUPS

2 cups fresh or frozen blueberries

2 cups water

1 cup sugar

1 teaspoon lemon zest

Simple syrup is commonly used to sweeten cocktails and other beverages. Try this blueberry version in place of sugar in iced tea or other favorite beverages.

1. Combine the blueberries, water, sugar, and lemon zest in saucepan over medium-high heat and bring to a boil. Reduce the heat to low and cook until thickened to the desired consistency, 15 to 20 minutes, or longer for a thicker syrup. Remove from the heat and let cool.

2. Strain out the berries and discard (or reserve them to make No-Waste Blueberry Butter, page 26), and transfer the syrup to a covered container. Refrigerate for up to 1 month.

Blueberry-Ricotta Pizza

with Caramelized Shallots and Blueberry Drizzle

MAKES ONE 12-INCH PIZZA

Drizzle

- 1 tablespoon Blueberry Simple Syrup (page 54)

- 1 tablespoon balsamic vinegar

Pizza

- 1 tablespoon extra-virgin olive oil

- 2 shallots, thinly sliced

- 1 flatbread pizza crust, fully baked

- ½ cup ricotta cheese, at room temperature

- ½ cup goat cheese, at room temperature

- ½ cup fresh blueberries

- Chopped fresh herbs (optional)

- Red pepper flakes (optional)

Whether served for lunch or dinner, or cut into small squares and served with cocktails, this pizza is a refreshing change of pace. Make it your own by sprinkling with your favorite herbs or adding a pinch of red pepper flakes before serving.

MAKE THE DRIZZLE

1. Whisk together the simple syrup and vinegar in a small bowl, then set aside.

MAKE THE PIZZA

2. Preheat the oven to 425°F (220°C).

3. Heat a small skillet over medium heat. When hot, add the oil and shallots. Cook, stirring frequently, until the shallots soften and begin to turn brown, 5 to 6 minutes. Remove to a paper towel to drain.

4. While the shallots are cooking, transfer the crust to a baking sheet and warm in the oven for 5 to 8 minutes.

5. Stir together the ricotta and goat cheese in a small bowl.

6. Remove the crust from the oven and spread the cheese mixture on top. Scatter the crust with the shallots and blueberries, then pour the drizzle over all. Return the pizza to the oven and bake for 7 to 10 minutes longer, or until the crust and cheese are warmed through. Top with herbs and pepper flakes, if using, then slice and serve warm.

Grilled Turkey and Cheese
with Blueberry-Onion Jam

MAKES 2 SANDWICHES

4 slices deli turkey breast

4 thick slices sourdough bread

2 ounces Brie cheese (or other melting cheese)

4–8 basil leaves

Blueberry-Onion Jam (page 49)

2 tablespoons butter, at room temperature

Gooey and delicious, this sandwich is hearty enough for a meal.

1. Pile the turkey breast on two pieces of bread. Top the turkey with the cheese and basil leaves. Spread some jam on the remaining two pieces of bread and place on top to make two sandwiches.

2. Heat a skillet over medium heat. When hot, add the butter and the sandwiches and sear until the sandwiches are crispy and golden on both sides, 2 to 3 minutes per side.

3. If the bread is sufficiently toasted but the cheese isn't melted enough, move the sandwiches to a microwave oven and heat for 10 to 15 seconds or to a hot oven for 4 to 5 minutes. Cut in half and serve warm.

Cinnamon–Brown Sugar Shortcake Biscuits

with Blueberries and Cream

MAKES EIGHT 2½-INCH BISCUITS

Biscuits

2 cups self-rising flour, plus more for shaping the dough

3 tablespoons firmly packed light or dark brown sugar

½ teaspoon ground cinnamon

1¼ cups heavy cream

Salted butter, melted

Decorating sugar or other large-grain sugar

Blueberries

2 cups fresh or frozen blueberries

¼ cup granulated sugar

Pinch of ground cinnamon

Pinch of ground nutmeg

Whipped Cream

½ cup granulated sugar

Pinch of salt

1½ cups heavy whipping cream

2 teaspoons vanilla extract

Individual sweet biscuits sliced open, drizzled with warm blueberries, and topped with whipped cream are what berry shortcake dreams are made of.

MAKE THE BISCUITS

1. Set an oven rack at the top level of the oven. Preheat the oven to 450°F (230°C). Line a baking sheet with parchment paper.

2. Whisk the flour, brown sugar, and cinnamon in a large bowl. Pour 1 cup of the cream into the flour and stir with a silicone spatula to quickly pull the flour into the cream. Mix just until the dry ingredients are moistened and the sticky dough begins to pull away from the sides of the bowl. Add a bit of the remaining cream, if necessary, to incorporate the remaining flour into the shaggy, wettish dough. If the dough is too wet, use more flour when shaping.

3. Lightly sprinkle a clean work surface with flour. Turn out the dough onto the floured surface and lightly sprinkle the top of the dough with flour. With floured hands, knead the dough two or three times until it just begins to come together. Fold the dough in half and pat it into a ½-inch-thick rectangle about 6 inches wide by 9 inches long. Repeat the folding and patting three times, using a little additional flour only if needed. Brush off any visible flour from the top of the final 6- by 9-inch rectangle. Dip a 2½-inch biscuit cutter into flour and cut out the biscuits, being careful not to twist the cutter.

4. Move the biscuits to the prepared baking sheet and brush with melted butter, then sprinkle with decorating sugar. Bake the biscuits on the top rack of the oven for 6 minutes, then rotate the baking sheet so that the front of the sheet is now turned to the back. Bake for 6 to 8 minutes longer, or until the biscuits are light golden brown. Transfer to a wire rack to cool.

PREPARE THE BLUEBERRIES

5. Heat the blueberries, granulated sugar, cinnamon, and nutmeg in a small saucepan over medium heat just until the sugar is melted. Remove from the heat and let cool.

PREPARE THE WHIPPED CREAM

6. Stir together the granulated sugar and salt in a large deep bowl. Add the cream and vanilla, and beat with an electric hand mixer until the cream has thickened and holds a firm peak, about 3 minutes. The cream may be made up to 8 hours ahead and stored in the refrigerator.

ASSEMBLE THE SHORTCAKES

7. Split the biscuits open and pile blueberries on the bottom half. Add a small dollop of cream, cover with the top of the biscuits, and finish with a dollop of cream.

Rich Blueberry Ripple Ice Cream

MAKES ABOUT 6 CUPS

- 5 egg yolks
- 1 cup sugar
- 2 cups heavy cream
- 1 cup milk
- 2 tablespoons vanilla extract
- ½ cup Small-Batch Easy Refrigerator Blueberry Jam or Blueberry-Lime Jam (page 28)

This classic vanilla custard-based ice cream is thick and rich, an excellent vehicle for the ribbon of blueberry jam. For a lighter base, omit the egg yolks and skip the heating.

1. Whisk the egg yolks and sugar together in a small heavy saucepan. Whisk in the cream and milk. Heat over medium heat, stirring every 30 seconds or so, scraping the bottom and sides of the pan, until the mixture reads 170°F (77°C) on an instant-read thermometer. Remove from the heat, stir in the vanilla, and pour through a strainer into a container. Cover and refrigerate the custard for at least 6 hours, preferably overnight.

2. Pour the chilled custard into a prepared ice cream churn and process according to manufacturer's directions. The ice cream will be soft. Transfer the ice cream to a shallow freezer-safe container. Spread the top with the blueberry jam and run a spatula through the jam into the ice cream to form the ripples. Freeze for at least 6 hours before serving.

Cinnamon-Brown Sugar Shortcake Biscuits with Blueberries and Cream (page 60) and Rich Blueberry Ripple Ice Cream

Picnic Blueberry Biscotti

**MAKES TWENTY-FIVE
½-INCH-THICK COOKIES**

- 2¼ cups all-purpose flour, plus more for dusting the work surface
- 1¼ cups granulated sugar
- 1¼ teaspoons baking powder
- ½ teaspoon salt
- 1 cup whole almonds, toasted and roughly chopped
- 2¼ teaspoons whole fennel seed, roughly chopped
- 2 eggs
- 1 tablespoon vanilla extract
- ¾ cup dried blueberries

A perfect car, boat, or picnic snack, these biscotti are dry cookies meant for dunking in coffee, tea, or wine. They travel well, as they are very sturdy. Although almonds are traditional, substitute any nut you may have on hand. Do try the fennel seed, though. Its faint aroma is essential to the experience.

1. Preheat the oven to 350°F (180°C). Line a baking sheet with parchment paper.

2. Whisk together the flour, sugar, baking powder, and salt in a large mixing bowl until thoroughly combined, at least 30 seconds.

3. Whisk the almonds and fennel seed into the flour mixture.

4. Stir in the eggs and vanilla, and stir until the dough comes together with no dry flour remaining. Stir in the blueberries.

5. Move the dough to a lightly floured work surface and knead the dough just enough to bring it together in a cohesive mass. It may seem as though it won't come together, but it will. Shape the dough into an 8-inch-long roll. Move the roll to the prepared baking sheet.

6. Using your hands, roll and lengthen the dough until it is 16 inches long. Flatten the dough until the roll is 4 inches wide (it should be about ½ inch thick).

7. Bake for about 25 minutes, or until the dough has puffed up a bit and is barely brown around the edges. Move the dough, still on the parchment paper, to a wire rack. Cool for 10 minutes.

8. Transfer the dough to a cutting board and cut the dough widthwise into ½-inch slices using a serrated knife. Move the slices back onto the parchment, cut-side up.

9. Bake the slices for 10 to 12 minutes, until lightly browned, then flip them over. Bake for 10 to 12 minutes longer, or until lightly browned and dry to the touch.

10. Transfer the biscotti to a wire rack and serve once completely cool. Store biscotti in an airtight container or ziplock bag for up to 3 months (keep out of direct sunlight so no moisture accumulates).

Homemade Blueberry Vodka

MAKES 1 (750 ML) BOTTLE

- 4 cups fresh or frozen blueberries
- ⅓ cup sugar
- 2 tablespoons water
- 1 (750 mL) bottle vodka (about 3 cups)

True blueberry flavor shines in this homemade blueberry vodka, making it a great choice for drinking in a blueberry martini (see page 68 for one of my favorite recipes). Plan ahead to infuse the vodka for five days, yielding the most flavorful results.

1. Cook the blueberries, sugar, and water in a small saucepan over medium heat until the blueberries are soft and release their juices, 8 to 10 minutes. Set aside to cool.

2. Combine cooled blueberry mixture and vodka in a large nonreactive bowl and cover loosely. Let stand at room temperature for 4 hours.

3. Cover and refrigerate for 5 days, or until the vodka has been infused with the blueberry flavor.

4. Strain out the solids by pouring the mixture through a fine-mesh strainer lined with cheesecloth into a glass jar or decanter. Gently press on the solids to extract a little more juice, but avoid squeezing as that releases more sediment. Discard the solids, or reserve them to make No-Waste Blueberry Butter (page 26).

5. Blueberry vodka keeps for 3 months in the refrigerator or for 6 months in the freezer in an airtight container.

Blueberry Martini

MAKES 1 COCKTAIL

½ cup ice cubes

1½ ounces Homemade Blueberry Vodka (page 67)

½ ounce sweet vermouth

1 tablespoon Blueberry Simple Syrup (page 54)

½ teaspoon freshly squeezed lemon juice

Lemon twist and fresh blueberries, for garnish (optional)

Flye Point in Brooklin, Maine, was settled in the late 1700s, and for more than 100 years a member of the Flye family has operated the Lookout Inn, located on the point, as a bed-and-breakfast. The bar serves a version of this simple blueberry martini every summer.

Place the ice cubes in a cocktail shaker. Add the vodka, vermouth, syrup, and lemon juice. Shake and strain into a martini glass. Garnish with a lemon twist and fresh blueberries, if desired.

Blueberry Whiskey Sour

MAKES 1 COCKTAIL

2 ounces rye or bourbon

1 ounce lime juice

1 egg white

½ ounce Blueberry Simple Syrup (page 54)

1 teaspoon Small-Batch Easy Refrigerator Blueberry Jam or Blueberry-Lime Jam (page 28)

3–4 ice cubes

3 drops Angostura bitters

This refreshing drink goes down easy! Enjoy this cocktail year-round — in winter for its stunning purple allure and in summer for its refreshing taste.

Combine the rye, lime juice, egg white, syrup, and jam in a cocktail shaker and vigorously shake for a few seconds. Add the ice, shake again just to cool the ingredients, and strain into a couple of cocktail glasses. Top with the bitters.

Blueberry Cobbler

MAKES 6 SERVINGS

⅓ cup unsalted butter

1 cup self-rising flour

½ cup granulated sugar
  or firmly packed light
  brown sugar

1 cup whole milk

4 cups fresh or frozen
  blueberries

My go-to dessert when I have people over for dinner is this easy cobbler. Assemble the cobbler just before sitting down to dinner and when dinner is over, the cobbler is ready. Your guests will be impressed! Using brown sugar will result in a darker cobbler.

1. Preheat the oven to 375°F (190°C). Place the butter in an 8- by 11-inch baking dish and put in the oven to melt.

2. Whisk the flour and sugar together in a small bowl until thoroughly combined, at least 30 seconds. Whisk in the milk. Remove the hot pan from the oven and pour the batter onto the hot butter. Sprinkle the blueberries over the top of the batter.

3. Bake the cobbler for 35 to 40 minutes, or until the batter has risen around the fruit, the top is light brown, and the edges are brown. The cobbler is done when a toothpick inserted in the center of the cobbler comes out clean (avoiding a blueberry). Serve warm. The cobbler can be made ahead, refrigerated, and reheated before serving.

Mini Linzer-Style Open Blueberry Hand Pies

DESSERT

MAKES 24 MINI HAND PIES

- 1 package (2-count) refrigerated piecrusts

  Flour, for dusting the work surface

- 1 egg

- 1 tablespoon water

- ½ cup Small-Batch Easy Refrigerator Blueberry Jam or Blueberry-Lime Jam (page 28)

  Decorating sugar or other large-grain sugar

These mini pie bites have the appeal of a Linzer cookie. They are easy to make using a store-bought piecrust.

1. Preheat the oven to 425°F (220°C). Line a baking sheet with parchment paper. Let the piecrusts rest at room temperature for about 15 minutes, or according to package directions.

2. Dust a work surface with flour, and lightly roll out the piecrusts. Using a 1¾-inch circular cookie cutter, cut out 24 circles in each crust (for a total of 48 circles) and move half of them to the prepared baking sheet. Using a ¾-inch circular cookie cutter, cut out the center of the remaining circles to make rings of dough. Gather the small rounds and set aside for another use (or dab with a bit of jam and bake as a tiny treat).

3. Whisk together the egg and water. Brush each pie circle on the parchment paper with the egg wash. Top with the pie rings. Brush the top of the rings with the egg wash.

4. Fill each depression with ½ teaspoon of the jam (it's easiest to do this in two dollops from a ¼-teaspoon measuring spoon). Using the tines of a fork, seal the edges around each pie. Sprinkle the rings with decorating sugar.

5. Bake for about 9 minutes, or until the tops are golden brown and the filling bubbles. Let cool for 10 minutes before serving. Store any remaining hand pies in the refrigerator.

Spiced Blueberry Slab Pie

MAKES ONE 13- BY 18-INCH
SLAB PIE, ABOUT 15 SERVINGS

---

2 packages (2-count)
refrigerated piecrusts
(4 total piecrusts)

½ cup granulated sugar

3 tablespoons cornstarch

2 teaspoons ground
cinnamon

¼ teaspoon ground nutmeg

Pinch of salt

8 cups fresh or frozen
blueberries

Flour, for dusting the work
surface

1 egg

1 tablespoon water

Decorating sugar or
other large-grain sugar

Serve this slab pie to feed a crowd at your next family reunion. The crust may tear in places when being rolled to size or transferred to the baking sheet, but it patches easily.

1. Preheat the oven to 425°F (220°C). Let the piecrusts rest at room temperature for about 15 minutes, or according to package directions.

2. Stir together the sugar, cornstarch, cinnamon, nutmeg, and salt in a large bowl. Add the berries and toss to coat. Set aside. (*Note:* If using frozen berries, add them just before pouring the filling into the pie.)

3. Dust a work surface with flour and place one piecrust on top of a second crust. Press and roll the piecrusts into a rectangle 14 inches wide by 19 inches long. Fold into fourths, move to a baking sheet, and line up the folded corner with the center of the baking sheet. Unfold and lift the edges of the piecrust to allow the crust to fall into the corners. Leave the overhanging edges and move the baking sheet to the refrigerator.

4. Add more flour to the rolling surface, if needed, and place the remaining piecrusts on top of each other on the flour. Press and roll into a rectangle 15 inches wide by 20 inches long. Leave whole, or cut into strips if making a lattice top.

5. Remove the piecrust from the refrigerator and pour the spiced blueberries evenly into the pie. Top with the second crust, tucking under at the edges, or decorate in a lattice pattern. Pinch or flute the edges as desired. If using a full top crust, cut slits in the top crust for venting.

6. Whisk together the egg and water in a small bowl and brush the top of the pie with the egg wash. Sprinkle with decorating sugar.

7. Bake for 20 minutes. Reduce the heat to 350°F (180°C) and bake for 35 to 40 minutes longer, or until the crust is browned and cooked through and the blueberries are bubbling. Cool, then cut into squares for serving.

Blue Ribbon Ginger-Lime Wild Maine Blueberry Pie

MAKES ONE 9-INCH PIE

Filling

¼ cup granulated sugar

Zest of 1 lime

¼ cup firmly packed light brown sugar

4 tablespoons cornstarch

1 teaspoon ground ginger

5–6 cups fresh wild Maine blueberries

Crust

2½ cups all-purpose flour, plus more for dusting the work surface

½ teaspoon salt

1 cup (2 sticks) salted butter, cut into ½-inch cubes

8–10 tablespoons ice-cold water

1 egg, lightly beaten

2 tablespoons decorating sugar or other large-grain sugar

This pie, which won first prize in the Blue Hill Fair in Maine in 2019, is everything wonderful about blueberries, all nestled in a flaky all-butter piecrust. Beginners need not fear this dreamy dough, shared with me by my friend, the cookbook author and pie maven Cathy Barrow. Return the dough to the refrigerator to chill down whenever you think things aren't going the way they should. It is inevitable that blueberry juice will bubble up out of the slits in the dough. That is part of the charm of a blueberry pie.

MAKE THE FILLING

1. Use your fingers to rub the granulated sugar and lime zest together in a small bowl until thoroughly combined. Whisk in the brown sugar, cornstarch, and ginger. Place the blueberries in a large bowl and toss with the cornstarch mixture until the berries are evenly coated. Set aside.

MAKE THE CRUST

2. Place the flour and salt in a food processor. Pulse 2 or 3 times to mix. Distribute the butter cubes evenly over the flour. Pulse 15 times. Add 4 tablespoons of the cold water. Pulse 10 times. Add 4 more tablespoons cold water and pulse 5 times. Grab a pinch of dough and squeeze it together. If it crumbles, add 2 more tablespoons water to bring the dough together with another pulse or two. Turn out the dough mixture onto a floured board. Knead slightly to form a cohesive dough. Divide the dough in half and form into two 5-inch disks, wrap in plastic wrap, and refrigerate for at least 1 hour.

ASSEMBLE THE PIE

3. Preheat the oven to 425°F (220°C).

4. Remove the crusts from the refrigerator and let rest for 10 minutes. Dust a work surface and rolling pin with flour. Roll out one disk by rolling from the center out to the edge, picking up the rolling pin and beginning in the center each time, and turning the dough a quarter turn after each roll, until the dough is roughly 1 inch larger than what will line the pie pan. Move the dough gently to the pie pan. Repeat the rolling process with the second disk.

5. Fill the pie with the blueberry mixture and top with the second dough. Trim away excess dough and use it to make a decorative braid for the rim of the pie. Seal the dough edges with a dab of water and decorate as desired. Vent the top crust with at least four slits. Brush the top crust with the beaten egg. If this process has warmed up the pie-crust, move the whole pie to the refrigerator to firm up the dough, for about 20 minutes.

6. Transfer the pie to a rimmed baking sheet and bake for 20 minutes. Reduce the heat to 350°F (180°C) and bake for 30 minutes longer. Sprinkle the pie with decorating sugar and bake for another 10 minutes, or until browned as desired. Let cool completely before cutting.

Fresh Blueberry Pie

MAKES ONE 9-INCH PIE

1 refrigerated piecrust

6 cups fresh blueberries, plus more for garnish (optional)

1½ cups sugar

1 teaspoon salt

6 tablespoons cornstarch

½ cup water

2 tablespoons unsalted butter

2 tablespoons lemon juice

2 cups heavy whipping cream

Take advantage of blueberry season with this fresh blueberry pie loaded with whipped cream, as seen in diners all across blueberry-loving states.

1. Bake the piecrust in a 9-inch pie pan according to package directions. Set aside to cool.

2. Mix 3 cups of the blueberries, 1 cup of the sugar, the salt, and the cornstarch in a large saucepan. Add the water and cook over medium-high heat until the mixture comes to a boil. Cook, stirring occasionally, for 2 minutes, or until thick.

3. Remove the pan from the heat and stir in the butter and lemon juice. Cool to room temperature, then mix in the remaining 3 cups berries. Pour the blueberry mixture into the cooled piecrust.

4. While berry mixture is cooling, whip the cream and the remaining ½ cup sugar in a large deep bowl using an electric hand mixer until stiff peaks form, about 3 minutes.

5. Pile the whipped cream over the pie and refrigerate until firm, about 2 hours. When serving, garnish the cut slices with additional fresh berries, if desired.

Skillet Blueberry Upside-Down Cake

MAKES ONE 9- OR 10-INCH CAKE

1½ cups all-purpose flour

2½ teaspoons baking powder

½ teaspoon salt

1 cup (2 sticks) unsalted butter, at room temperature

¾ cup granulated sugar

2 eggs

2 teaspoons vanilla extract

⅔ cup milk

¾ cup firmly packed light or dark brown sugar

1½ cups fresh or frozen blueberries

Developing this recipe took me straight back to my grandmother's kitchen, complete with her cast-iron skillet. Memory lane never tasted so good.

1. Set an oven rack in the center of the oven. Preheat the oven to 350°F (180°C).

2. Whisk together the flour, baking powder, and salt in a small bowl until thoroughly combined, at least 30 seconds.

3. Beat ¾ cup of the butter and the granulated sugar together in large deep bowl with an electric hand mixer until light in color and fluffy, 3 to 4 minutes. Beat in the eggs and vanilla for 30 seconds.

4. Add the flour mixture to the butter mixture in thirds, alternating with half the milk, beating until combined, and scraping the bottom of the bowl between each addition. Set aside.

5. Melt the remaining ¼ cup butter in a 10-inch cast-iron skillet over medium heat. Stir in the brown sugar. When incorporated, remove from the heat and sprinkle with the blueberries.

6. Pour the batter over the blueberries in the skillet. Move the skillet to a baking sheet and transfer to the hot oven. Bake for 30 to 40 minutes, or until golden and a toothpick inserted in the center comes out clean (avoiding a blueberry).

7. Run a thin offset spatula or knife around the edge of the cake to loosen it, and let the cake cool for just 5 or so minutes. Place a serving platter over the cake, then invert the platter and skillet so that the loosened cake drops onto the platter. Cut and serve warm.

Sour Cream–Blueberry Bundt Cake
with Lemon Glaze

DESSERT

**MAKES ONE 10- TO 12-CUP
BUNDT CAKE**

Cake

1 cup granulated sugar

Zest of 2 lemons

1 cup firmly packed light or
dark brown sugar

1 cup (2 sticks) unsalted
butter, at room temperature

4 eggs

1 teaspoon vanilla extract

2½ cups all-purpose flour, plus
more for dusting the pan

2 teaspoons baking powder

1 teaspoon salt

1 cup sour cream

2 cups fresh or frozen
blueberries

Glaze

1½ cups confectioners' sugar

¼ cup freshly squeezed
lemon juice

Appropriate for any occasion, this glorious, dense, and delicious Bundt cake serves a crowd.

MAKE THE CAKE

1. Set an oven rack at the lowest level of the oven. Preheat the oven to 350°F (180°C). Spray or grease the inside of a 10- to 12-cup Bundt pan with oil and dust with flour.

2. Use your fingers to rub the granulated sugar and lemon zest together in a large deep bowl until thoroughly combined. Whisk in the brown sugar. Add the butter and beat with an electric hand mixer until light in color and fluffy, 3 to 4 minutes. Beat in the eggs one at time, beating after each addition until incorporated. Beat in the vanilla.

3. Whisk together the flour, baking powder, and salt in a small bowl until thoroughly combined, at least 30 seconds.

4. Add the flour mixture to the butter mixture in thirds, alternating with half the sour cream, beating until combined and scraping the bottom of the bowl between each addition. Gently fold in the blueberries.

5. Spread the batter in the prepared pan, and tap the pan on the counter once or twice to remove any air bubbles. Move the pan to a baking sheet and place on the bottom rack in the hot oven.

6. Bake for 65 to 70 minutes, or until the cake is golden brown on top, begins to pull away a bit from the sides of the pan, and a toothpick inserted in the center comes out clean (avoiding a blueberry). Let cool on a wire rack for 1 hour. Invert the cake out of the pan and onto the rack to finish cooling. Transfer the cake to a serving platter. Or, to freeze the cake, wrap the unglazed cake well and store in the freezer for up to 3 months, then glaze at serving time.

MAKE THE GLAZE

7. Mix together the confectioners' sugar and lemon juice in a medium bowl. If the glaze is too thick, add a little water until the desired consistency is achieved. Drizzle the glaze over the cooled cake and serve.

Blueberry Layer Cake

with Lemon Curd Filling and Cream Cheese Frosting

MAKES ONE 9-INCH THREE-LAYER CAKE

Cake

- 3 cups all-purpose flour, plus more for dusting the pan
- 1 tablespoon baking powder
- ½ teaspoon salt
- 1¼ cups granulated sugar
- Zest of 2 lemons
- 1 cup (2 sticks) unsalted butter, at room temperature
- ½ cup firmly packed light or dark brown sugar
- 4 eggs, at room temperature
- 2 cups buttermilk
- ½ cup freshly squeezed lemon juice
- 2 teaspoons vanilla extract
- 1½ cups fresh blueberries
- 1 cup Lemon Curd (next page)

Frosting

- 12 ounces cream cheese, at room temperature
- ½ cup (1 stick) unsalted butter, at room temperature
- 1 teaspoon vanilla extract
- 4 cups confectioners' sugar
- 1–2 tablespoons heavy cream or milk, if needed

A mid- to late-summer birthday begs to be celebrated with this gorgeous confection. Bright with lemon flavor throughout, this triple-layer cake is a memorable blueberry-studded treat for any occasion.

MAKE THE CAKE

1. Preheat the oven to 350°F (180°C). Spray or grease and flour three 9-inch round cake pans, line the bottoms with parchment paper, and spray or grease and flour the paper.

2. Whisk together the flour, baking powder, and salt in a medium bowl until thoroughly combined, at least 30 seconds.

3. Use your fingers to rub the granulated sugar and lemon zest together in a large deep bowl until thoroughly combined. Add the butter and brown sugar, and beat with an electric hand mixer until light and fluffy, about 4 minutes. Add the eggs one at a time, beating after each addition.

4. Mix the buttermilk, lemon juice, and vanilla together in a small bowl or measuring cup.

5. Add the flour mixture to the butter mixture in thirds, alternating with half the milk mixture, beating until combined and scraping the bottom of the bowl between each addition.

6. Spoon the batter into the three pans, tap each on the counter to release air bubbles, and move to the hot oven. Bake for 22 to 25 minutes, or until lightly browned and springy to the touch and a toothpick inserted in the center comes out clean. Transfer the layers to a wire rack. Run an offset spatula or a knife around the edge of each pan to loosen, cool for 10 minutes, then invert each pan onto the rack. Peel off the paper and reinvert the layers to fully cool. Once cool, trim the layers with a serrated knife to achieve a flat top.

MAKE THE FROSTING

7. While the layers are cooling, beat the cream cheese, butter, and vanilla together with an electric hand mixer in a large deep bowl until smooth. Add the confectioners' sugar and beat until smooth and creamy. If the frosting is too thick, add a bit of the cream. Cover and refrigerate until ready to frost the cakes.

ASSEMBLE THE CAKE

8. Using an offset spatula, spread lemon curd between the layers. Add a third of the blueberries each to the bottom and middle layers. Coat the top and sides of the cake with frosting. Decorate the bottom edge of the cake with the remaining one-third blueberries and serve. Refrigerate any leftovers.

LEMON CURD

MAKES 1½ CUPS

5 egg yolks

1 cup sugar

½ cup (1 stick) unsalted butter, at room temperature

½ cup freshly squeezed lemon juice, plus more as needed

3 tablespoons lemon zest, plus more as needed

1. Lightly whisk the egg yolks in a heavy saucepan or double boiler. Whisk in the sugar and butter, then the lemon juice.

2. Stir the egg mixture with a silicone spatula over low heat until thick but still falling easily from a spoon, 5 to 10 minutes, making sure to scrape the sides and bottom of the pan. The temperature should register approximately 170°F (77°C) on an instant-read thermometer, and the mixture should be saucy. If too thin, carefully cook for a few minutes longer. (If the mixture simmers at the edges of the pan, quickly strain; it will be usable if smooth and no egg bits remain.)

3. Stir the zest into the curd. Season to taste with more juice or zest. Remove from the heat and cool. Store in the refrigerator in a tightly covered jar for up to 4 weeks.

Blueberry-Lemon Icebox Loaf Cake

DESSERT

MAKES ONE 9- BY 5-INCH LOAF

2¼ cups fresh or frozen blueberries

½ cup sugar

2 tablespoons freshly squeezed lemon juice

3 cups heavy whipping cream

¾ cup Lemon Curd (page 87)

9–11 graham cracker squares

1 teaspoon lemon zest

This loaf cake needs to sit in the freezer overnight. It can be hard to wait a day for this heavenly goodness, but it's worth it. Homemade lemon curd is divine, so if you'd like to make it for this recipe, prepare a batch a day ahead, cook the blueberries ahead as well, and refrigerate both until cold. Cooled or cold ingredients are best for this recipe.

1. Line a 9- by 5-inch loaf pan with two sheets of plastic wrap. Lay one sheet horizontally and one sheet vertically inside the pan, each extending at least 4 inches beyond the rim of the pan.

2. Place 1 cup of the blueberries in a small saucepan. Smash the berries with a potato masher or other implement. Add another 1 cup of blueberries, the sugar, and lemon juice, and bring to a boil. Reduce the heat to low and simmer for 5 minutes. Remove from the heat to cool.

3. Whip 2 cups of the cream in a large deep bowl using an electric hand mixer until stiff peaks form, about 3 minutes. Fold ¼ cup of the lemon curd into the whipped cream and transfer the bowl to the refrigerator until needed.

4. When ready to assemble, coat the bottom of the prepared loaf pan with a layer of whipped cream. Spread 3 graham crackers with some of the remaining lemon curd and place on top of the cream. Drizzle half of the blueberry sauce over the graham crackers. Repeat again using ¼ cup lemon curd in total, and top with a final layer of graham crackers and more whipped cream. Fold the plastic wrap over the top of the cream and lightly press down to compress the layers. Move the loaf to the refrigerator and leave overnight, or up to 24 hours.

5. When ready to serve, whip the remaining 1 cup cream to soft peaks, and fold in the remaining ¼ cup lemon curd. Unmold the loaf cake by opening the plastic wrap and inverting the cake onto a platter. Remove the plastic wrap.

6. Coat the outside of the loaf with the whipped cream and top with the remaining ¼ cup blueberries. Sprinkle with the lemon zest, cut, and serve cold.

Instant Pot Blueberry Swirl Cheesecake

MAKES ONE 7-INCH CHEESECAKE

Compote

- 1 cup fresh or frozen blueberries
- ¾ cup sugar
- 1 teaspoon lemon juice
- 1 teaspoon cornstarch

Crust

- 1¼ cups crushed graham crackers (about 8 rectangles)
- 1 tablespoon sugar
- 4 tablespoons unsalted butter, melted

Filling

- 8 ounces cream cheese, at room temperature
- 1 cup ricotta cheese, at room temperature
- ¼ cup sour cream
- 2 eggs
- 1 tablespoon cornstarch
- 2 teaspoons lemon juice
- 1 teaspoon vanilla extract

Do you find it too stressful to watch a cheesecake baking in the oven? A 6- or 8-quart Instant Pot pressure cooker cures that worrisome feeling by sealing the cake inside where you can't peek, and the pressure cooking ensures that the cake will be perfectly cooked every time. Do allow time for the ricotta and cream cheese to come to room temperature before beginning.

1. Fold a 24-inch-long piece of foil in half lengthwise and in half again lengthwise, to form a foil sling 3 inches wide and about 24 inches long. Place a wire rack or metal trivet on the bottom of the Instant Pot insert.

MAKE THE COMPOTE

2. Combine the blueberries, sugar, lemon juice, and cornstarch in a small saucepan over medium heat. Bring to a boil, reduce the heat to low, and simmer until the mixture thickens, about 5 minutes. Set aside to cool, then refrigerate.

MAKE THE CRUST

3. Place the graham crackers in a ziplock plastic bag. Crush with a rolling pin or your hands until fine crumbs form. Transfer the crumbs to a small bowl and stir in the sugar. Pour the melted butter over the crumb mixture and combine thoroughly with a fork. Press the crumbs into the bottom of a 7-inch springform pan, covering the bottom and at least 1 inch up the sides. Use the bottom of a glass to smooth the surface. Transfer the pan to the freezer until needed.

MAKE THE FILLING

4. Beat the cream cheese, ricotta, and sour cream together in a large bowl with an electric hand mixer until just combined. Add the eggs one at a time, beating and scraping the bowl after each addition. Stir in the cornstarch, lemon juice, and vanilla.

ASSEMBLE THE CAKE

5. Remove the crust from the freezer and pour the cheesecake filling into the crust. Top with ½ cup of the blueberry compote and use a knife to swirl the compote into the filling. Smooth the top with an offset spatula, if needed.

6. Pour 1 cup of water into the Instant Pot insert. Place the springform pan in the center of the foil sling and move the sling and pan into an 8-inch cake pan. (If your Instant Pot is smaller than 8 quarts, wrap the bottom of the springform pan with aluminum foil instead.) Move the cake pan onto the rack inside the insert. Tuck the sling into the sides.

7. Seal the top of the pot and cook on high pressure for 15 minutes. Allow for a natural release for 15 minutes, then switch to manual release. Remove the lid carefully to avoid dripping moisture onto the cheesecake. Use the sling to remove the springform pan. Dab the top of the cheesecake with paper towels if necessary to remove any collected moisture. Move the cheesecake to the refrigerator for at least 6 hours, but preferably overnight.

8. When ready to serve, remove the cheesecake from the refrigerator. Run an offset spatula around the inside edge of the pan. Open the springform pan and transfer the cheesecake to a serving platter. Top the cheesecake with the remaining blueberry compote. Cut and serve.

Blueberry-Lemon-Basil Granita

MAKES 6 SERVINGS

- ⅔ cup water
- ½ cup sugar
- ⅔ cup freshly squeezed lemon juice
- Zest of 1 lemon
- 10 medium fresh basil leaves, finely chopped, plus whole leaves for garnish (optional)
- 3 cups frozen wild blueberries, defrosted

Vibrant, icy, and refreshing, this sweet-sour granita cools off a hot summer day. Made with frozen wild blueberries, it's the best of both worlds — healthy antioxidants and dessert.

1. Bring the water and sugar to a boil in a medium saucepan over medium-high heat. Reduce the heat to low and simmer until the sugar is completely dissolved. Remove from the heat and carefully stir in the lemon juice, lemon zest, and basil. Let cool for about 30 minutes.

2. Meanwhile, purée the blueberries in a blender. Add the cooled syrup and blend again.

3. Pour the mixture into a shallow glass baking dish and transfer to the freezer. Stir the mixture with a fork every 45 minutes until firm, about 4 hours. When ready to serve, scrape the surface with a fork until granular crystals form. Scoop the granita into bowls and serve, garnished with basil leaves, if desired.

ACKNOWLEDGMENTS

Single-subject books are incredibly rewarding to write, as they are a deep-dive with a single focus. They have become my passion! Thank you to my acquisitions editor, Deanna Cook, who chose me to kick off this new fruit series for Storey Publishing. My editor, Sarah Guare, has corrected all of my mistakes and my copy editor, Paula Brisco, makes me look so much smarter than I am. I remain indebted to you all.

My agent, Lisa Ekus, introduced me to Deanna over lunch, saying she thought we should know each other because "who knows?" Thank you for being my biggest cheerleader.

If it were not for Nathalie Dupree, I would never have known I could have a career in food. Thank you for opening up my world.

My family has shared my love of blueberries for so many years. I will treasure my memories of my children, Norman and Rachel, picking wild blueberries on Caterpillar Hill in Maine as wee little ones. I look forward to the next generation of blueberry pickers.

If it were not for Anne and Heyward Siddons, I never would have ventured to the Blue Hill Peninsula to discover the tall pines and rocky blueberry barrens. Returning to Brooklin now for more than 25 years, my gratitude knows no bounds. I miss you both so very much.

My husband, Cliff, provides me with a lifestyle that allows me to write for pleasure. He is my champion, promoter, defender, and advocate. I am grateful to you, sweetie, and am happy to still be in love these 33 years later.

To the farmers who till the soil, tend the fields, and produce my beloved berry, you are the rock stars I admire. Thank you for bringing such bounty to my table.

And to that blueberry farmer from Florida who came through my life after a very low period, just when I needed to be told that I was worthy, I thank you. It worked.

INDEX

Page numbers in *italics* indicate photos.

B

bacon
  Spinach, Blood Orange, Goat Cheese, and Bacon Salad, 42, *43*
basil
  Granita, Blueberry-Lemon-Basil, 96, *97*
  Salsa, Blueberry and Red Onion, *32*, 33
  Turkey and Cheese, Grilled, 58, *59*
Biscotti, Picnic Blueberry, 64–65, *65*
Bread, Blueberry-Pecan, 30, *31*
Butter, No-Waste Blueberry, 26, *26*, *27*
Buttermilk Blueberry Pancakes, 16, *17*
Buttermilk Blueberry Soup, 34, *35*
Buttermilk Corn Muffins, Gluten-Free Blueberry, 44, *45*

C

cake
  "Boy-Bait," 1954 Blueberry, *8*, 9
  Bundt Cake, Sour Cream–Blueberry, 84–85, *85*
  Cheesecake, Instant Pot Blueberry Swirl, 92–93, *93*, *94–95*
  Coffee Cake, Blueberry, 6, *7*
  Icebox Loaf Cake, Blueberry-Lemon, 90–91, *91*
  Layer Cake with Lemon Curd Filling and Cream Cheese Frosting, Blueberry, 86–87, *89*
  Upside-Down Cake, Skillet Blueberry, 82, *83*
cheese. *See also* cream cheese
  Blueberry, Watermelon, Feta Cheese, and Mint Salad, 38, *39*
  Pizza with Caramelized Shallots and Blueberry Drizzle, Blueberry-Ricotta, 56, *57*
  Turkey and Cheese, Grilled, 58, *59*
  Wild Blueberry, Horseradish, and Blue Cheese Spread, 36, *37*
Chicken and Blueberry Salad, Warm Grilled, 46, *47*
Chicken with Blueberry Chutney, Whole Roast, 52, *53*
Chutney, Blueberry, 52, *53*
Cobbler, Blueberry, 70, *71*
Coffee Cake, Blueberry, 6, *7*
cream cheese
  Cheesecake, Instant Pot Blueberry Swirl, 92–93, *93*, *94–95*
  Layer Cake with Lemon Curd Filling and Cream Cheese Frosting, Blueberry, 86–87, *88–89*

D

Danishes, Make-Ahead Blueberry Jam Breakfast, 22–23, *23*, *24–25*
Doughnuts, Blueberry Cinnamon-Spiced, *18*, 19
drinks
  Martini, Blueberry, 68, *69*
  Muddle, Blueberry, Bourbon, and Mint, 54, *55*
  Shrub, Blueberry, 40, *41*
  Smoothie, Rachel's Blueberry-Matcha, 12, *13*
  Vodka, Homemade Blueberry, 66, *67*
  Whiskey Sour, Blueberry, 68, *69*

E

eggs/egg yolks
  French Toast Casserole, Make-Ahead Blueberry-Pecan, 14, *15*
  Ice Cream, Rich Blueberry Ripple, 62, 63
  Lemon Curd, 87, 88

F

French Toast Casserole, Make-Ahead Blueberry-Pecan, 14, *15*

G

ginger
  Chutney, Blueberry, 52, *53*
  Ginger-Lime Wild Maine Blueberry Pie, Blue Ribbon, 76–77, *77*, *78–79*
  Muffins, Jumbo Bakery-Style Ginger-Blueberry, 20, 21
Gluten-Free Blueberry Buttermilk Corn Muffins, 44, *45*
graham crackers
  Cheesecake, Instant Pot Blueberry Swirl, 92–93, *93*, *94–95*
  Icebox Loaf Cake, Blueberry-Lemon, 90–91, *91*
Granita, Blueberry-Lemon-Basil, 96, *97*

H

horseradish
  Wild Blueberry, Horseradish, and Blue Cheese Spread, 36, *37*

I

Ice Cream, Rich Blueberry Ripple, 62, 63

J

jam
  Blueberry-Lime Jam, 28–29, 72, *73*
  Blueberry-Onion Jam, *48*, 49, 58, *59*
  Danishes, Make-Ahead Blueberry Jam Breakfast, 22–23, *23*, *24–25*
  Refrigerator Blueberry Jam, Small-Batch Easy, 28, 72, *73*

L

lavender
  Lemonade, Blueberry-Lavender, 12, *13*

lemons/lemon juice/lemon zest
Bundt Cake, Sour Cream–
Blueberry, 84–85, *85*
Butter, No-Waste Blueberry, 26,
26, *27*
Chicken with Blueberry Chutney,
Whole Roast, 52, *53*
Granita, Blueberry-Lemon-Basil,
96, *97*
Icebox Loaf Cake, Blueberry-
Lemon, 90–91, *91*
Layer Cake with Lemon Curd Filling
and Cream Cheese Frosting,
Blueberry, 86–87, *88*
Lemonade, Blueberry-Lavender,
12, *13*
Lemon Curd, 87, *88*
Refrigerator Blueberry Jam, Small-
Batch Easy, 28
Simple Syrup, Blueberry, 54, *55*
lime juice/lime zest
Blueberry-Lime Jam, 28–29
Ginger-Lime Wild Maine Blueberry
Pie, Blue Ribbon, 76–77, *77*, *78–79*
Whiskey Sour, Blueberry, 68, *69*

M

Maple Syrup, Blueberry, 16, *17*
Martini, Blueberry, 68, *69*
mint
Blueberry, Bourbon, and Mint
Muddle, 54, *55*
Blueberry, Watermelon, Feta
Cheese, and Mint Salad, 38, *39*
Muffins, Gluten-Free Blueberry
Buttermilk Corn, 44, *45*
Muffins, Jumbo Bakery-Style Ginger-
Blueberry, 20, *21*

N

nuts
Biscotti, Picnic Blueberry, 64–65,
65
Bread, Blueberry-Pecan, 30, *31*

French Toast Casserole, Make-
Ahead Blueberry-Pecan, 14, *15*
Smoothie, Rachel's Blueberry-
Matcha, 12, *13*
Wild Blueberry, Horseradish, and
Blue Cheese Spread, *36*, *37*

O

onions
Blueberry-Onion Jam, *48*, *49*, 58,
59
Salsa, Blueberry and Red Onion,
32, 33
orange juice/orange zest
Doughnuts, Blueberry Cinnamon-
Spiced, 18, 19
Scones, Dried Blueberry-Orange,
10, *11*
Soup, Buttermilk Blueberry, 34, *35*
Spinach, Blood Orange, Goat
Cheese, and Bacon Salad, 42, *43*

P

Pancakes, Buttermilk Blueberry, 16, *17*
pie
Ginger-Lime Wild Maine Blueberry
Pie, Blue Ribbon, 76–77, *77*, *78–79*
Hand Pies, Mini Linzer-Style Open
Blueberry, 72, *73*
Pie, Fresh Blueberry, *80*, 81
Slab Pie, Spiced Blueberry, 74, *75*
Pizza with Caramelized Shallots and
Blueberry Drizzle, Blueberry-Ricotta,
56, *57*
Pork Tenderloin with Blueberry
Balsamic Mustard Glaze, Sautéed,
50, *51*

S

salads
Blueberry, Watermelon, Feta
Cheese, and Mint Salad, 38, *39*
Chicken and Blueberry Salad, Warm
Grilled, 46, *47*

Spinach, Blood Orange, Goat
Cheese, and Bacon Salad, 42, *43*
Salmon Fillets with Blueberry-Onion
Jam Glaze, *48*, 49
Salsa, Blueberry and Red Onion, 32, 33
Scones, Dried Blueberry-Orange, 10, *11*
shallots
Blueberry-Ricotta Pizza with
Caramelized Shallots and
Blueberry Drizzle, 56, *57*
Chutney, Blueberry, 52, *53*
Shortcake Biscuits, Cinnamon–Brown
Sugar, 60–61, *61*
Shrub, Blueberry, 40, *41*
Simple Syrup, Blueberry, 54, *55*
Smoothie, Rachel's Blueberry-Matcha,
12, *13*
Soup, Buttermilk Blueberry, 34, *35*
Sour Cream–Blueberry Bundt Cake,
84–85, *85*
Spinach, Blood Orange, Goat Cheese,
and Bacon Salad, 42, *43*

T

Turkey and Cheese, Grilled, 58, *59*

V

Vinaigrette, Blueberry, 42, *43*
Vodka, Homemade Blueberry, 66, *67*

W

watermelon
Blueberry, Watermelon, Feta
Cheese, and Mint Salad, 38, *39*
Whiskey Sour, Blueberry, 68, *69*

Y

yogurt
Chicken and Blueberry Salad, Warm
Grilled, 46, *47*
Doughnuts, Blueberry Cinnamon-
Spiced, *18*, 19
Smoothie, Rachel's Blueberry-
Matcha, 12, *13*